Burgh Island and Bigbury Bay

of Yesteryear

Chips Barber

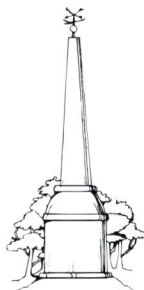

OBELISK PUBLICATIONS

OTHER TITLES IN THIS SERIES

Beesands and Hallsands of Yesteryear, *Cyril Courtney*
Beesands and Torcross of Yesteryear, *Cyril Courtney*
Ashburton of Yesteryear, *John Germon and Pete Webb*
The Teign Valley of Yesteryear, Parts I and II, *Chips Barber*
Brixham of Yesteryear, Parts I, II and III, *Chips Barber*
Pinhoe of Yesteryear, Parts I and II, *Chips Barber*
Kingsteignton of Yesteryear, *Richard Harris*
Heavitree of Yesteryear, *Chips Barber* • Ide of Yesteryear, *Mavis Piller*
Kenton and Starcross of Yesteryear, *Eric Vaughan*
Princetown of Yesteryear, Parts I and II, *Chips Barber*
Exmouth Century, Parts One and Two, *George Pridmore*
Exmouth of Yesteryear, *Kevin Palmer* • Littleham of Yesteryear, *Kevin Palmer*
Sampford Peverell of Yesteryear, *Bridget Bernhardt and Jenny Holley*
Sidmouth of Yesteryear, *Chips Barber* • Crediton of Yesteryear, *Victoria Labbett*
St Thomas of Yesteryear, Parts I, II and III, *Mavis Piller*
Whipton of Yesteryear, *Chips Barber and Don Lashbrook*
Dawlish of Yesteryear, *Chips Barber* • Torquay of Yesteryear, *Leslie Retallick*
Devon's Railways of Yesteryear, *Chips Barber*
Kingskerswell of Yesteryear, *Chips Barber and John Hand*
Chagford of Yesteryear, *Chips Barber* • Dartmoor of Yesteryear, *Chips Barber*
Okehampton of Yesteryear, *Mike and Hilary Wreford*
Lympstone of Yesteryear, *Anne Scott* • Exminster of Yesteryear, *Chips Barber*
Whitchurch of Yesteryear, *Chips Barber* • Dartmouth of Yesteryear, *Chips Barber*

OTHER TITLES ABOUT THIS AREA

Around & About Burgh Island and Bigbury-on-Sea, *Chips Barber*
Around & About Hope Cove and Thurlestone, *Chips Barber*
Around & About Salcombe, *Chips Barber* • The Great Little Totnes Book, *Chips Barber*
Along The Avon, *Chips Barber* • The South Hams in Colour, *Chips Barber*
The Story of Hallsands, *Chips Barber* • From The Dart to The Start, *Chips Barber*
Walks in The South Hams, *Brian Carter*
Walk The South Hams Coast–Dartmouth to Salcombe, *Chips Barber*
Walk The South Hams Coast–Salcombe to Plymouth, *Chips Barber*
Newton Ferrers and Noss Mayo, *Chips Barber*
We have over 180 Devon titles. For a full list please send an SAE to
Obelisk Publications, 2 Church Hill, Pinhoe, Exeter EX4 9ER

ACKNOWLEDGEMENTS
Many thanks to Steve Salter and Judith Marchant for their help on this book.

First published in 2004 by
Obelisk Publications, 2 Church Hill, Pinhoe, Exeter, Devon
Designed and Typeset by Sally Barber
Printed in Great Britain
by Avocet Press, Cullompton, Devon

Burgh Island
and
Bigbury Bay

of Yesteryear

"Wish you were here!" "Wonderful weather!" "Having a marvellous time!" Part of any holiday ritual has traditionally been to send bright and breezy holiday greetings home to one's family and friends, courtesy of a few scribbled lines on a picture postcard. This little book draws heavily on such views, largely from the early part of the last century, together with early local guide books, to illustrate how Burgh Island, and the various small resorts along the Bigbury Bay shoreline, looked in the past. The featured places include Hope Cove, South Milton, Thurlestone, Bantham, Challaborough and Bigbury-on-Sea.

In the scene below, one lady is happy to pose outside the attractive thatched cottages at Hope Cove, whilst another resident seems to be a little camera-shy. The postcard on which this image appeared was posted on 6 December 1906 and noted that this was a very quiet spot at 'the end of nowhere'. In those days and at that time of the year, it would have been!

Cottages at Hope.

Burgh Island and Bigbury Bay of Yesteryear

Bigbury Bay has long been a graveyard for ships and shipwrecked mariners. Opposite (top) is the *Jebba*. Having safely travelled from the west coast of Africa, with a cargo of bananas, ivory, palm oil and other items, the vessel went aground near Hope Cove on 18 March 1907. Operated by the Coastguard from the high cliffs, a rocket apparatus lifted 38 people to safety, whilst the remaining 117 on board were rescued by local fishermen. The next picture is dated 1936; scribbled on the back was: "Hope Cove – The 'new' part from the new road."

The scene above was taken from the privately-owned cliff known as The Shippen. Inner Hope (shown in the bottom picture opposite) lies to the right of the scene; the former lifeboat house is only partly visible. Written on the back of the 1938 postcard was: "This part of the country thrills me more each time I come down. There is still such a vast amount of unspoilt beauty." According to a 1914 Devonshire directory: *The inhabitants of Hope Cove are chiefly engaged in fishing; quantities of crabs and lobsters are caught. Here is a lifeboat station; the boat, called the* Alexandra*, is endowed and was presented to the Royal Lifeboat Institution in 1877 by the Grand Lodge of Freemasons of England, on the occasion of the return of their grand master, His late Majesty King Edward VII then Prince of Wales; a large boat house was also erected on the sands.* Today there is no lifeboat, Salcombe being the nearest station. On the next page there are three views of Hope Cove, the top two looking in the opposite direction to the bottom one.

Burgh Island and Bigbury Bay of Yesteryear

Thurlestone Rock, which gives the nearby village its name, is an extremely resistant red conglomerate stack standing on Devonian clay slates. This was written about it in 1864: *It stands about thirty feet in height, and the hole is twenty feet high by ten broad. At ebb tide it is sometimes left dry, but at the flood, the waves often wash over it… It has been stated as a fact that within the memory of some persons recently living, this isolated rock formed a portion of the mainland, and that cows had been seen grazing upon it. If this is the case, the sea must have great power, for the space between the cliffs and the rock is of very considerable extent. The noise made by the wind rushing through the archway is sometimes heard many miles away, and when it is perceptible at Kingsbridge it is regarded as the fore-runner of storms of rain.*

Ye Olde Village Shoppe, South Milton.

South Milton lies just over a mile inland from Thurlestone Rock. It occupies a location towards the head of the marshy valley leading down to the sea. The 1910 county directory listed Mrs Sarah Miller as the sole shopkeeper and postmistress in this village. There was also more of a police presence in South Milton at that time, as is evidenced by the police house on the right of the picture below.

South Milton

LINKS HOTEL AND BRIDGE, THURLESTONE.

This stream, which has some deep pools, reaches the beach not far from Thurlestone Rock. The bridge enables a dry crossing for those who walk the coast path.

The sender of the postcard below, showing Thurlestone village, informs us that the weather on 1 September 1913 was 'glorious'. When this picture was taken, the village was little more than one long street. At that time the shopkeeper was William Hingston Pound, and the sub-postmaster was John Elworthy Sherriff. Since then the village has grown, more than doubling in population between 1901 and 1981.

Thurlestone Village

Above is the former Links Hotel at Thurlestone. As one would expect from its name, it overlooked the golf course, which was designed by Harry S. Cott. The golf course was founded in 1897 by the local doctor, a brewer and a solicitor. One of them was named Beer!

Although similar to the one at the bottom of this page, the middle picture was taken at a different time – but can you spot which came first by looking at the changes? The middle view is earlier, there being fewer properties vying for sea views.

The middle picture on this page shows the Village Inn. This was the original Thurlestone Hotel, before the present hotel was built to the right of it. This postcard was sent 'home' to Chatham on 20 June 1907. Below, the Avon is seen greeting the sea between Bantham and Bigbury-on-Sea. This card was posted from Kingsbridge to Copenhagen on 18 August 1930. As the message on the back was written mostly in Danish, the only recognisable words (to me) are "Glorious Devon!" How right the sender was!

These two pictures of Bantham – a hamlet perched on a bluff above the Avon – were taken years apart: the one above dating back to 1880, the one below to 1908. In the early years of the twentieth century, Richard Brooking was the landlord of the Sloop Inn, which is just visible on the far left. The combined village shop and post office was run by the ever-busy John Elworthy Sherriff, who was also a baker and confectioner. Both pictures are taken looking in the same seawards direction; the faint outline of Burgh Island (then known as Borough Island) is just discernible in the distance.

The message on the back of the early 1950s card above congratulated Devonshire people on being 'charming' (of course they are!). The sender also had the good fortune to have enjoyed a month of fine, sunny weather at 'beautiful Bantham'.

The scene below is a stone's throw away from the one above; it shows the quaint thatched boathouses of this small river port.

Burgh Island and Bigbury Bay of Yesteryear

BIGBURY FROM BANTHAM.

Above are the sand dunes at Bantham. The view looks towards Burgh Island, which can be spied on the left-hand side of the scene, its gleaming white hotel an obvious landmark.

The picture below also looks across the dangerous mouth of the River Avon, where the mingling river and sea waters swirl and eddy.

We have now crossed the Avon, but only just. Taken from close to Sharpland Point, the sandy beach shown towards the left of the view is Sedgewell Cove, used in recent times for the filming of several sequences for the BBC television series *Down to Earth*.

The scene below shows the road running into Bigbury-on-Sea – a relatively modern settlement by Devonshire standards.

GENERAL VIEW, BIGBURY ON SEA.

Burgh Island and Bigbury Bay of Yesteryear

The excellent photograph above (taken at low water) was published by M. M. Chubb of the post office, Bigbury-on-Sea, at a time when this was a much smaller settlement. Houses now cover the hillside, peering over each other for a glimpse of Burgh Island and the silver, shiny sea of Bigbury Bay. The layout of this settlement is unique for Devon: it has an American-styled grid pattern of roads. A close look reveals that the current Burgh Island Hotel has yet to be built. It now stands to the left of the wooden summer house, which was constructed in the late nineteenth century for George H. Chirgwin (1854–1922), a famous music hall performer. It was an ideal retreat for someone who sought privacy from his adoring public; when he acquired the island, it had four fishermen's cottages and the pub. He was a master of several musical instruments; it is said that he could 'bash out a tune' on almost anything, even teapots! For his minstrel comedy act, he adopted the stage-persona of 'the White-Eyed Kaffir'. His striking make-up consisted of a black-face with a solid white-painted diamond around his right eye. In 1900 he was billed as 'the Funniest Man on Earth'. At this time the only road down to Bigbury-on-Sea was little more than a cart track. (The first surfaced road was constructed in 1906.) In his last years, 'GHC' owned the Swan Hotel at Shepperton, which he bought as a retirement investment. Visitors today may choose to stay in the Chirgwin Suite on the top floor of the much grander island hotel.

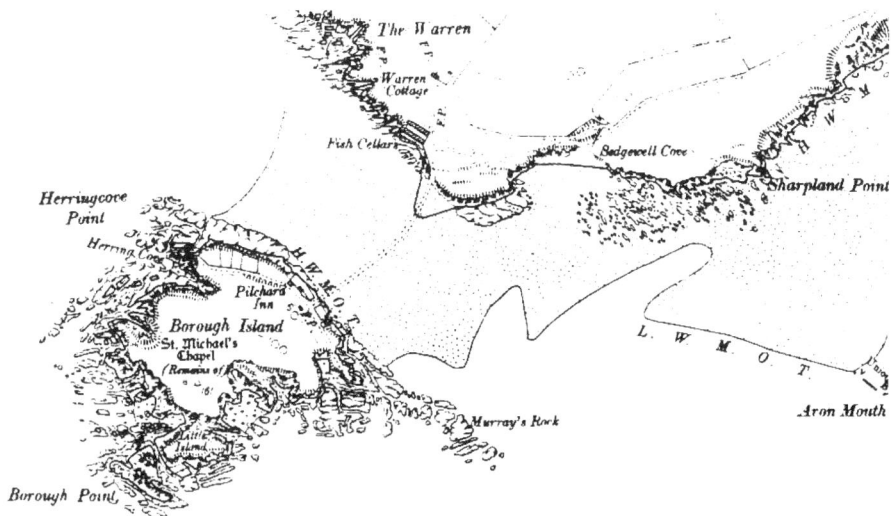

The map extract above is from the late 1890s and shows how little development had taken place by that time. The only dwelling shown at Bigbury-on-Sea, a name not featured on the map, was Warren Cottage. The island's name is given as 'Borough' but has since, perhaps through laziness or poor spelling, corrupted to Burgh Island. A detective of place-names would also be able to make a reasoned guess as to the past importance of the fishing industry: Herringcove Point, the Pilchard Inn and the 'Fish Cellars' are a giveaway.

The aerial view below was taken from high above Challaborough. The sandy causeway leading to the 'part-time island' can be seen on the left-hand side of the picture whilst a path, which resembles a grand prix circuit around the island's perimeter, is clearly visible. From the air it looks fairly flat, but it is a steady climb to reach the huer's hut on the island's summit.

Burgh Island and Bigbury Bay of Yesteryear

Burgh Island

Treasure here X

Cove

Pilchard Inn

Lobster Fishing

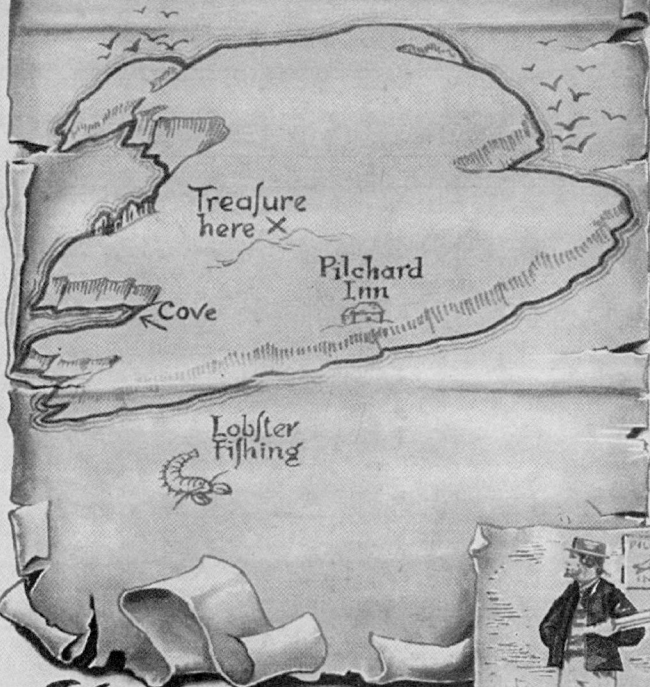

Ye Treasure of Tom Crocker

THE HOTEL, BURGH ISLAND, BIGBURY-ON-SEA.

In the 1930s, the Burgh Island Hotel produced a 16-page guide book; apart from promoting its attractions, it also gave a potted history and geography lesson on the island. The cover is reproduced on the opposite page; as well as the island, it refers to Tom Crocker, a former villain who, allegedly, buried his ill-gotten gains there. The drawings that appear on the following pages have been taken from that early publication.

The hotel was built in the late 1920s by Archibald Nettlefold (the N of the famous engineering firm GKN) after he heard that the island was for sale, together with its small wooden 'hotel' (1896). He engaged Matthew Dawson, the talented Paris-trained architect, to design him a 'Great White Palace'.

In steel and concrete, using straight lines and the occasional curve, the four-storeys-high, dazzlingly white-painted hotel gave the island a completely new look.

It has entertained many famous guests, including Agatha Christie, Noel Coward, The Beatles, Amy Johnson, Winston Churchill, the Mountbattens, and Edward, Prince of Wales, who stayed there with Wallis Simpson. If only its walls could talk…

Here are some extended extracts and illustrations from the 1930s guide: *The modern 'Treasure Island,' so might Burgh Island be called. Only a few miles from Plymouth it lies – nestling under the warm red cliffs of Devon and washed by the sea of the English Channel, and the Atlantic Ocean.*

Shaped like a fish, this fact is immortalized in the name of the Island's only Inn – Pilchard Inn, built in 1395.

Burgh Island – steeped in folk lore of the dim past, the one-time haunt of Pirates and Smugglers (led by none other than the notorious Tom Crocker) is an island of romance, adventure and treasure.

Tom Crocker, Prince of Smugglers, cleverly evaded capture for many years, until eventually he was trapped by the Customs men. A pirate flag and a carving bearing the likeness of Crocker (both of which can be seen in the Pilchard Inn) commemorate the event.

Gone are the smugglers – gone are the pirates. The bold, bad men who step ashore to-day, come in search of the greatest treasure of modern days – health and rest.

Burgh Island now possesses the finest Hotel of its kind in Britain. It is built on modern lines, and here the visitor will find luxury and comfort comparable with that available in the finest West End hotel, whilst surrounded by the veritable treasure of antiquity of which the island boasts. The perfect blending of ancient and modern.

Exquisitely furnished, Burgh Island Hotel defies comparison. It is unique – not only in association with the past, but with the discriminating contact with the present. It is unique in that it is not 'just another hotel,' but a complete holiday resort in itself.

For those in search of the perfect rest-and-relaxation holiday, Burgh Island offers the ideal, whilst to visitors from America and Overseas it proffers everything that is usually lacking in the average English hotel.

The 'grounds' of the Hotel are the Island itself. Visitors have uncontrolled access to every part – with one exception – For over 700 years one family have owned the fishing rights of a small corner of the Island. The present generation consists of three brothers, Jack, Syd and Jim.

To them the present Island owner has granted those rights – until they die. So they continue, uninterrupted, their lobster and sea fishing. Their methods of fishing are the same as used by their ancestors through the centuries. Here are real men of the sea – a modern reminder of those men who founded England's maritime greatness in bygone ages.

Not the least interesting room in this modern Hotel is the Ganges Room, built from the stem of the top deck of the famous HMS Ganges, which was broken up at Plymouth in 1930 after many years of yeoman service to the British nation. She was the last sailing ship to serve as a seagoing flagship to the British Navy.

This room overlooks a wonderful natural swimming pool – Swallow Pool, access to which is gained from the sun-porch which borders the south side of the Hotel. Steps lead to the sandy little beach and pool, once famous as a 'cove' of Tom Crocker in plying his illicit trade.

Where contraband once was landed, now lounge sun-bathers from Mayfair, enjoying perfect bathing by day, moonlight or electric light, in the pool which boasts two tides a day, and whose waters are warm even in late Autumn and early Spring.

Everything necessary for your enjoyment and entertainment is here.

Specially laid tennis courts and the glorious sea-breezes combine to put an extra 15 on everybody's game, whilst one of the most beautiful and popular golf courses on the mainland is owned by the Hotel, and visitors have all rights of the Course.

Magnificent views can be obtained from the hotel roof-gardens where, if you prefer you may find amusement in deck-tennis, shuffleboard or midget-golf.

Sea-fishing, climbing, exploring, roof-gardens, dancing and talking pictures are further attractions which have brought the discriminating English-man to this perfect holiday resort. The tone, comfort, excellent food and wines of the hotel are things about which to dream when the holiday is over and always demand an early repetition.

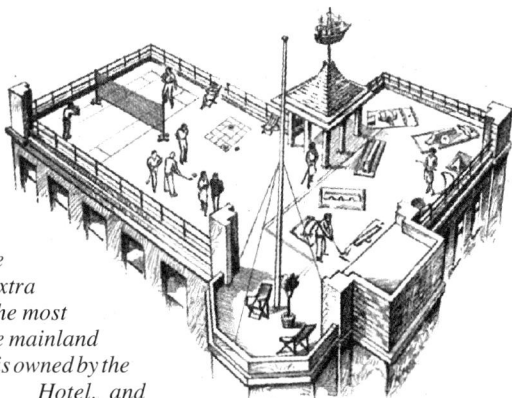

'Burgh Island via Plymouth' – will soon be a recognized route for visitors from America, for the Island is 'on the doorstep' of those making Plymouth their port. Moreover, from London (Paddington) it is only four hours' journey...

Burgh Island is a gem of nature – and to the Modern it offers every comfort science and invention can provide whilst never losing touch with the 'romance' of the bygone ages.

The entrance to the Hotel is protected by curved wind-vanes which make a pleasant semi-circular shelter for windy days.

This illustration of the Lounge shows but a corner of that comfortable apartment, but serves to show the position of the Ganges Room, which overlooks the bathing pool. The Dining Room, with its shaded lights and beautiful decorations, is one of the most charming rooms in the Hotel.

One wall is completely occupied by deep French windows leading on to the Dining Verandah.

Quiet and restful, the circular card-room strikes just the right note for a rubber of bridge. The Billiard Room also, with its large alcove and recessed fireplace, makes an irresistible appeal to lovers of the game.

The bedrooms represent sheer comfort. Beautifully appointed, many lead on to balconies from which magnificent views are obtained. Every bedroom is fitted with wash-hand basins with hot and cold water.

There is an adequate number of bathrooms, but private suites, comprising Double Bedroom, Sitting Room, and Bath Room, are also obtainable.

The food, appointments and service of the Hotel are all that can be desired, and the Management appreciate that visitors are on holiday, using every endeavour to make their stay as carefree and enjoyable as possible, according to the individual taste of each guest.

The views on this page are similar in that they were both taken from the island looking towards the mainland. However, their dates are almost half a century apart.

In the past Bigbury-on-Sea had its own, typically upbeat, 24-page guide book. About a quarter was given over to relevant details of the immediate district, of which these are some of the finer points. As you will see, some of the comments would be regarded as a bit bizarre today. The word 'windy' is carefully avoided! *Delightfully situated, facing South, open to Bigbury Bay and the English Channel. The Climate is sunny, bracing and invigorating, the rainfall below the average. The subsoil is sandy, the ground at all times in good condition. The climate can be further judged by the vegetation that thrives there. The Mesembryanthemum (or Hottentot Fig) which is a native of the coast of Australia, grows luxuriantly. This plant is very tender, proving conclusively, that there is little or no frost at Bigbury-on-Sea.*

The Estate is laid out on the Garden City plan, every bungalow having good views of the sea and the surrounding country. They are of varying designs, and of a most comfortable type. The pleasure of living in a bungalow can only be fully appreciated by those who are fortunate enough to obtain one. There are several private Hotels and Boarding Houses, all reasonably near the sands. There is an abundant supply of pure water, obtained from several springs and pumped into a large reservoir. The Estate receives its supply of Electricity from Torquay. The bungalows are fitted with all necessary electric conveniences.

There is a frequent 'bus service from North Road Station, Plymouth. Time tables, post free, 4d, apply J. J. Chubb, Bigbury-on-Sea, Agent for the Western National Omnibus Co Ltd...

VIEW FROM BURGH ISLAND, BIGBURY ON SEA.

Burgh Island and Bigbury Bay of Yesteryear

Another 'bus service is also operated between Bigbury-on-Sea and Kingsbridge during the summer, a distance of 10 miles. This service connects up with the branch line of the GWR from South Brent, which is on the main line of the Company's system to Plymouth. For a real restful holiday, Bigbury-on-Sea is probably unequalled, its bracing, breezy and invigorating air, is a revelation to visitors, and the care-free 'do-as-you-please' tone is much appreciated.

As a Summer Resort, Bigbury-on-Sea is somewhat unique. Although situated on the south coast of Devon, it stands well forward in the celebrated Bigbury Bay, and catches every breath of air, so that during the hottest weather, the temperature is never oppressive, and its bracing effect is equal to any on the north coast.

As a Winter Resort it is making a name, the temperature being equable, and rarely showing those extremes of heat and cold, found on many parts of the coast. Its freedom from frosts and snow, and the amount of winter sunshine is often mentioned by visitors. During recent winters, many families have occupied bungalows, and expressed themselves pleased with the winter conditions.

As a Health Resort it is second to none. The healthy appetite, and glowing cheek, the sprightly walk and cheerfulness of spirit, are found by the most depressed in a few hours, without being able to account for it... Salmon are found in the River Avon, and during the season (May to September) the Salmon Pool under Folly Farm is drawn at high and low tide daily, many fine fish being secured. Visitors find much interest in watching the work, and often assist in drawing the seine. Bass are caught in considerable numbers, in the estuary of the same river, whilst pollack, conger, chad, and bream frequent the rocks. Mackerel and herrings, especially the former visit the bay in quantities. Great sport can be had for young and old in catching lance or sand eels, on the sandy edges of the river. Fishing (except salmon) is without restriction. Crabs and lobsters can be obtained from the local fishermen...

Smugglers' Caves. Like most parts of Devon and Cornwall, Bigbury-on-Sea has its memories of the past. Several caves exist in this neighbourhood. The finest one of roomy capacity, with a front entrance, almost unobserved, with partial subterranean passages, is situated at Warren Point. The cave is difficult of access, but well worth a visit. It will be found just under the Devil's Spy Glass (a large hole leading from the land to the sea, and formerly used for landing smuggled goods). It must, however, be visited at low tide, as the sea enters the cave at high tide.

The seaweed collector can gather some very beautiful specimens in various colours, which are well worth mounting. When on a visit to Bigbury-on-Sea, pebble hunting should not be omitted. Some good specimens of semi-precious stones can be found. If there are no flaws in the pebbles they are worth cutting and polishing. Many beautiful samples have been secured by visitors.

Burgh Island is immediately opposite, and approached from Bigbury-on-Sea, from which it is situate a quarter of a mile across the sands, for about six hours daily. There is a fully licensed inn on the island, probably one of the oldest in the kingdom. Mr A. Nettlefold, the owner, recently erected a large and very comfortable hotel on the side of the island... There is an excellent eighteen-hole golf course, covering 130 acres, total length, 5,760 yards. Laid out by Messrs Hawtrey and Taylor... The Bigbury-on-Sea Garage have accommodation for cars, they also supply petrol. Repairs executed. Cars for hire.

When Mr Nettlefold died, his widow extended the hotel and labelled it 'the finest hotel west of the Ritz'. It prospered from the 1930s to the early 1950s, but then fell on harder times. In 1955 it ceased trading as a hotel. For the next thirty years its various owners offered self-catering facilities, but only for the peak summer months. The building began to suffer from the ravages of the weather experienced in this exposed spot and by the mid-1980s had become run-down. In 1985, Beatrice and Tony Porter bought the island and set about slowly restoring the building to its former art deco glory. It became a hotel again in 1988. Having owned the island for quite a few years, the Porters sold it in 2001. It was bought by Tony Orchard and Deborah Clark.

The early Bigbury-on-Sea guide book contained some interesting advertisements but relied heavily on businesses from larger neighbouring places such as Modbury, Aveton Gifford and Kingsbridge to support it. A telephone call could be made on Bigbury-on-Sea 2, to reserve accommodation at the Colinton Hotel shown here. Situated about a hundred feet above sea-level, fine views of the Bay were enjoyed. By adding an extra number, a caller to Bigbury-on-Sea 22 could book to stay at the Korniloff Private Hotel, which had croquet, five garages and electric light amongst its many facilities. For those who wished to commit themselves to a longer stay, the City Expert Building Company, which had branches in Plymouth and also at Bigbury-on-Sea, was willing to give free estimates and professional advice: "Bungalows erected at Bigbury-on-Sea at very reasonable prices." For those who required the land for such a project, Mr J. J. Chubb (tel. no. 26) was on hand to sell building plots. During the Second World War he used his organisational skills and local knowledge to find billets for evacuees.

Above is a picture of the former Seaside Stores. Just below it, a large part of the former bus garage later became a mock fishing village. Within the complex, but beyond 'the village street', lay the Tom Crocker bar. Although the building was an ugly one, the view from it, across to the island, was wonderful. Having shown obvious signs of wear and tear, the buildings on this site were demolished in the 1990s to be replaced by luxury apartments. A new purpose-built beach shop, which now caters for the needs of those who flock to the resort on warm summer days, was also constructed nearby.

This picture from 1998 shows the complex a short time before it was demolished.

The view below shows Bardens' Tea Rooms. The county directory for 1910 lists Alfred Douglas Bardens as being landlord at the Royal Oak in Bigbury, whilst Mrs Christina Bardens performed the same role at the Pilchard Inn on 'Borough Island'. By 1914 she had relinquished this post, the wind of change seeing Alfred D. Breeze at the helm. According to a later guide book, Mrs C. Bardens ran 'Beach View' at Challaborough, which offered guests "the best in fresh fish and local lobsters as well as indoor sanitation". Meanwhile J. Bardens was proprietor of the Bigbury Filling Station and General Stores.

During the Second World War, what is now the Bay View Café was commandeered for use as a school. Mr and Mrs Adamson, from Eltham in London, along with Judith their young daughter, relocated to Devon. At first, in 1940, the Adamsons stayed at Diptford higher up the Avon valley, but in March 1941 they arrived in Bigbury-on-Sea to set up a school for 5-to-14-year-olds. There was only a single toilet at the back to serve the needs of all, but a second was added to relieve the situation. The small hut-like building on the right was the infants' school. Mr Adamson taught in the glass-roofed restaurant. On sunny days the temperature reached an uncomfortable level so the windows had to be opened as wide as was possible. In sharp contrast, the winters brought such ferocious winds that Mrs Adamson had a single door created at the back of the building, as at times it was almost impossible to open the wind-battered side door.

Opposite are two photographs of the evacuees. In the top one, Mr Adamson is seen with his senior pupils; in the other, children are enjoying the beach.

Although the children had been evacuated for their own safety, they were not completely immune from the effects of the conflict. A barrage balloon, which had been placed over Plymouth, broke loose and eventually found its way into Bigbury Bay, where it grounded in the Avon estuary. It then slowly deflated. In March 1942, a Flying Fortress returning from a bombing mission at St Nazaire also came down into the water at the estuary mouth. The crowd which gathered to watch this exciting episode was treated to the spectacle of the crew members clambering aboard their rubber dinghy, then rowing to safety on the Bantham side of the river. The plane was later dismantled.

When Plymouth, about sixteen miles away, was blitzed, the western night sky at Bigbury-on-Sea was greatly illuminated. There were no purpose-built air-raid shelters here, but on the grassy bank between the two school buildings there were extensive rabbit holes. Mr Adamson organised the older children to enlarge them. If machine gunners threatened, he would blow a whistle and in a trice they could seek safer shelter.

The Burgh Island Hotel was used as a recuperation centre by the RAF. On one dramatic occasion, it was bombed. A great cloud of asbestos dust enveloped the island; observers mistook it for a thick sea mist. Most of the damage was confined to the entrance hall; it was most fortunate that the troops had vacated the building an hour earlier, in order to catch the tide.

According to the local paper: *"The annual sports of the Bigbury-on-Sea Evacuee School were held at Sedgewell Sands on July 29th, in splendid weather. This year the children from Bigbury village school, under Miss Leadbetter, the mistress, joined the party. All the features were much enjoyed, every child taking part in one or more of the events. The prizes were distributed by Mrs L. N. Adamson, senior. The proceedings, which were a great success, were organised by Mr R. B. B. Adamson, Mrs Adamson and Miss Burgess."* The events included flat races, skipping, 'Bunny Hop', 'Jack and Jill', 'Pebble', 'Shoe', 'Fishing', 'Kangaroo', 'Bathing' and 'Ball and Spoon' – eggs were in short supply and certainly not to be wasted.

A short way inland from Bigbury Bay, the Journey's End pub at Ringmore is unusual in that it is named after a 1920s play of the same name: R. C. Sherriff wrote it whilst staying there. This 1939 picture shows him reading a manuscript with Gabriel Pascal (right) for the 1941 film version of *Major Barbara*. The original intention was to film in places between Salcombe and Plymouth, but the rapid escalation of Second World War hostilities rendered this impossible. Just a few years after the war, the pub attracted some national media coverage under the headline "A Wonder Piglet – On 3 Bottles of Brandy". The story was told by an unnamed *Sunday Dispatch* reporter: *Born three weeks before he was expected, Chapelcombe Incredible was kept alive on a diet of brandy, glucose and milk to become Devon's wonder-piglet. After consuming three bottles of brandy he has not only confounded veterinary surgeons by surviving but, say the experts, he has*

Burgh Island and Bigbury Bay of Yesteryear

the makings of a champion. With flannel next to skin, and his home on top of the kitchen cooker at the Journey's End at Ringmore-with-Kingston, near Plymouth, Incredible has been nursed night and day. Son of a champion, he was the only one of ten piglets to live. Incredible was cared for by Mrs M. B. Paterson, mother of 16-year-old Alan Paterson, who had started farming in partnership with Mr Jay Pullyblank. Mrs Paterson injected a mixture of brandy, glucose and milk down Incredible's throat with a fountain pen filler. Vets said that she was wasting her time. After his third bottle of brandy – and still thriving – Incredible was taken off the treatment. Promptly he protested by going off his feed. Then he was induced to take glucose and milk. He has not looked back since. Now 8 inches high, he is the life and soul of the local hostelry and as lively as a cricket. He is deep chested, with perfect black and white markings.

Opposite (bottom) and on this page are views of Challaborough, the small resort close to Bigbury-on-Sea. These photographs were taken long before the mass of caravans spread far up the steep-sided valley. The picture below shows the coastline to the west as far as Stoke Point, the western limit of Bigbury Bay. The stream that flows into the sea here was once notorious. It seems that, just above the top of the beach, a number of visitors had the great misfortune to fall in it; fortunately, it's shallow. There used to be a sign beside it along the lines of '21 people have fallen in so far, don't be number 22!' The bridge has now been replaced by a safer structure.

126. CHALLABOROUGH.

Above is part of Challaborough. The stream which caused problems can be spied wending its way across the sandy beach.

The aerial photograph below is from the mid-1990s and shows Burgh Island and the mouth of the Avon.

As we reach the end of this trip down memory lane, please bear in mind that the postcard you send home from your holiday could one day be featuring in another book like this. So, please write clearly… and say something interesting!

Burgh Island and Bigbury Bay of Yesteryear